Tender Thoughts for Couples

Tender Thoughts for Couples

Wisdom for Keeping Your Marriage on the Same Page

CLARA HINTON

New Leaf Press

First printing: January 2002

Copyright © 2002 by New Leaf Press. All rights reserved.
No part of this book may be used or reproduced in any man-
ner whatsoever without written permission of the publisher
except in the case of brief quotations in articles and reviews.
For information write: New Leaf Press, Inc., P.O. Box 726,
Green Forest, AR 72638.

ISBN: 0-89221-520-8
Library of Congress Number: 2001098911

Unless otherwise noted, all Scripture references are from the
New American Standard Bible. Other versions used are the
New International Version (NIV) and the New Century Ver-
sion (NCV).

Printed in the United States of America

Please visit our website for other great titles:
www.newleafpress.net

For information regarding author interviews, contact the
publicity department at (870) 438-5288.

Dedication

This book is affectionately dedicated to my husband, John, the only person who makes my life complete.

Acknowledgments

My most sincere gratitude to the staff at New Leaf Press who worked endless hours with me to make a difficult task seem easy. My special thanks to Jim Fletcher, Roger Howerton, and Brent Spurlock for taking the pages of this book and making them come alive. An eternal thanks to my publisher, Tim Dudley, who believes in God's plan of marriage so much that he said, "Let's go with the book!"

Introduction

Marriage is the most intriguing, most mysterious, and most gratifying union any man and woman can ever experience. Keeping a marriage alive and thriving can be hard work, taking lots of focused effort and endless energy. Only when God is at the very heart of a marriage can the two become one in body, mind, and soul according to God's perfect plan.

It is my prayer that these *Tender Thoughts for Couples* will encourage your marriage to remain joyfully forever on the same page.

Lovingly,
Clara Hinton

For *Her*

"Words from the mouth of a
wise man are gracious, while
the lips of a fool consume
him." Eccles. 10:12

Learn to communicate;

it takes lots of time.

Tell your wife how you feel;

your wife is not a mind reader.

"People's thoughts can be like a deep well, but
someone with understanding can find the
wisdom there." Prov. 20:5; NCV

6

"Do not let the sun go
down on your anger."
Eph. 4:26

End an argument fast.
    Seal it with a kiss.

Do not carry arguments into
    another day; forgive quickly.

"He who is slow to anger
is better than the
mighty." Prov. 16:32

For Him

"Then the Lord God said, 'It is not good for the man to be alone. I will make a helper who is right for him." Gen. 2:18; NCV

Men think differently than women,
Learn that fact early on.

When your wife makes absolutely
no sense, love her anyway.

"The heart of her husband trusts
in her" Prov. 31:11

*Fix one special meal a week
just for him.*

Make each day special

in some way.

"People ought to enjoy every day
of their lives, no matter how long
they live." Eccles. 11:8; NCV

For Him

9

When you quarrel, don't call home to mother. Mothers have long memories and active tongues.

When your wife is upset, go to her, hold her, and let her know the two of you can work things out.

Neatness is not as important to most men as women, so relax some in this area.

Empty the garbage without being asked.

"Do all things without grumbling or disputing." Phil. 2:14

For Him

11

"There is an appointed time for
everything. And there is a time
for every event under heaven."
Eccles. 3:1; NCV

Buy him a calendar and
mark all special dates on
it in bold lettering.

Remember special days with
a card, a flower, a nightie,
or some bubble bath.

"Oil and perfume make the
heart glad." Prov. 27:9

"When I was a child, I used to speak as a child, think as a child, reason as a child; when I became a man, I did away with childish things." 1 Cor. 13:11

Expect immaturity for a while.
It takes time to grow up.

Be gentle with your wife.
Remember — you're
growing up together.

"A gentle answer turns away wrath." Prov. 15:1

For Him

13

Enjoy laughter with your husband. It helps put problems in perspective.

Have a sense of humor, but do not make light of real problems.

"In the day of prosperity be happy, but in the day of
adversity consider — God has made the one as well as
the other so that man may not discover anything that
will be after him." Eccles. 7:14

*Don't expect the honeymoon
to last forever.*

Learn to enjoy your work.

"Whatever your hand finds to
do, verily do it with all your
might." Eccles. 9:10

For Him

"Have you found honey?
Eat only what you need."
Prov. 25:16

Don't make him your entire life;
that puts a drain on a marriage.

Give your wife some time to do girl
things with her friends.

"Do not withhold good from those
to whom it is due, when it is in your
power to do it." Prov. 3:27

"Indeed, there is not a righteous man
on earth who continually does good and
who never sins." Eccles. 7:20

Learn real fast to
overlook a lot.

Remember — this is new for both
of you. Make allowances.

"I don't understand . . . the way
a man and woman fall in love."
Prov. 30:18–19

For Him

17

"*The tongue of the wise makes knowledge acceptable.*" Prov. 15:2

Gentle words get the job done a
lot quicker than harsh words.

Angry words benefit no one, but
hearing the words "I love you"
can move mountains.

"*A man will be satisfied with good by the fruit of his words.*"
Prov. 12:14

Bickering is inevitable; try to end a bicker in its early stages before it becomes a fight.

Learn to say
"I love you"
often.

For Him

"What you say can mean life or death.
Those who speak with care will be
rewarded." Prov. 18:21; NCV

*Never laugh at your
husband's dreams.*

Life is made of dreams;
dream together.

"A good person can look forward to
happiness." Prov. 10:28

"Make every effort to keep the
unity of the Spirit through the
bond of peace." Eph. 4:3; NIV

Teach your husband the
art of cuddling.

A warm hug says more
than a thousand words.

"There is a time to hug."
Eccles. 3:5; NCV

21

"I held on to him and would not let him go." Song of Sol. 3:4

Hold hands often.

Walking hand-in-hand
is a reminder of how
your love began.

"My lover's left hand is under my head, and his right arm holds me tight." Song of Sol. 8:3

"Cease from anger and forsake
wrath; do not fret, it leads only to
evil doing." Ps. 37:8

Argue a point,

not the person.

Never let an argument separate
you from the one you love.

"Malign no one, be uncontentious,
gentle, showing every consideration
for all men." Titus 3:2

For Him

For Her

"And do not neglect doing good and sharing; for with such sacrifices God is pleased." Heb. 13:16

Husbands love surprise gifts
— no matter how small.

A small unexpected act of kindness
means much more than a big
gift given from guilt.

"In all things, show yourself to be an
example of good deeds." Titus 2:7

24

*Plan outings for just
the two of you.*

Take your wife

on a

romantic walk.

For Her

"He who covers a transgression seeks love." Prov. 17:9

Don't put him down.
And never put him down
in front of someone.

Compliment your wife to others.

"Give her the reward she has earned; she should be praised in public for what she has done." Prov. 31:31

"As a ring of gold in a swine's snout,
so is a beautiful woman who lacks
discretion." Prov. 11:22

*Learn to keep a
private talk private.*

Don't share your wife's
intimate thoughts
with others.

"He who goes about as a talebearer
reveals secrets, but he who is trustworthy
conceals a matter." Prov. 11:13

For Him

27

"Worry is a heavy load, but a
kind word cheers you up."
Prov. 12:25; NCV

Talk before going to bed.

Remember that your wife is more
interesting than the evening news.

"Husbands, in the same way be considerate as
you live with your wives, and treat them with
respect." 1 Pet. 3:7; NIV

"And which of you by being anxious
can add a single cubit to his life's
span?" Matt. 6:27

*Do not rob your marriage of joy today
by worrying about problems that do
not have an immediate solution.*

Make your wife laugh.
It will help lighten the
mood of the day.

"Rejoice with those who
rejoice, and weep with those
who weep." Rom. 12:15

For Him

29

"He who guards his mouth and his tongue guards his soul from trouble." Prov. 21:23

Always take the time to think before you speak.

Once angry words are spoken, they are never easily forgotten.

"An angry person causes trouble; a person with a quick temper sins a lot." Prov. 29:22; NCV

Crying during the first year of marriage is normal. Remember — you are making major adjustments each day.

If possible,
call your wife once each day
just to say "I love you."

For Him

31

"Among the young men, my lover is like an apple tree in the woods! I enjoy sitting in his shadow; his fruit is sweet to my taste." Song of Sol. 2:3; NCV

Treat him like you did when you were still dating. He will seem more exciting.

Kiss like you did before you were married.

"May he kiss me with the kisses of his mouth! For your love is better than wine." Song of Sol. 1:2

"Don't be too right, and don't be
too wise. Why destroy yourself?"
Eccles. 7:16

Allow room for some doubts.
It's all part of the first year.

It is easier to see the best,
when you expect the best.

"Now faith is being sure of what we
hope for and certain of what we do
not see." Heb. 11:1; NIV

For Him

Focus on his good points and diminish the bad.

Look at her
through eyes of love.

"How beautiful you are, my darling, how beautiful you are! Your eyes are like doves." Song of Sol. 1:15

"*He who restrains his words has knowledge.*" Prov. 17:27

Be a patient listener.
What your husband has to say
is important, too.

Listen with your heart
as well as your ears.
Your wife needs all of you.

"Be kind to one another, tenderhearted, forgiving each other, just as God in Christ also has forgiven you." Eph. 4:32

Your husband can survive almost anything — except negligence. Tenderly care for him.

Just as a rose needs tender care, your wife needs your gentle touch every day.

"Husbands love your wives, just as Christ also loved the church and gave Himself up for her." Eph. 5:25

"For the husband is the head of
the wife as Christ is the head of
the church." Eph. 5:23

A husband who honors God
is the most cherished
of all blessings.

A wife who respects God
is worthy of your everything.

"Charm is deceptive, and beauty is
fleeting; but a woman who fears the
Lord is to be praised." Prov. 31:30

For Him

For Her

"And let us not lose heart in doing good." Gal. 6:9

Surprise your husband
by preparing his
favorite breakfast.

Serve your wife breakfast
in bed at least once a month.

"But through love serve one
another." Gal. 5:13

38

"You are so handsome, my
love, and so pleasant!"
Song of Sol. 1:16; NCV

*Remind yourself how happy
you felt with this man before
you were married.*

Remember why this was
the woman of your choice.

"May the Lord make your love
increase and overflow for each
other." 1 Thess. 3:12; NIV

For Him

"A joyful heart is good
medicine." Prov. 17:22

Plan time with other couples.
It is healthy to laugh and be
with others your own age.

Allow room for friends.
They will enrich
your marriage.

"If one falls down, his friend can help him up."
Eccles. 4:10; NIV

> *"A joyful heart makes a cheerful face, but when the heart is sad, the spirit is broken."* Prov. 15:13

Laugh together often.

All work and no play
makes a husband
a very distant person.

> *"For where your treasure is, there will your heart be also."* Luke 12:34

"Come, my beloved, let us go out into the country, let us spend the night in the villages." Song of Sol. 7:11

Plan time away from the house or apartment together. Home seems great after some time away.

Watch a sunrise
together.

"Sunshine is sweet; it is good to see the light of the day." Eccles. 11:7; NCV

"And if we have food and covering, with
these we shall be content." 1 Tim. 6:8

*Don't expect every luxury in life
all at once.*

Be a responsible provider.

"But if anyone does not provide for his
own, and especially for those of his
househould, he has denied the faith, and is
worse than an unbeliever." 1 Tim. 5:8

43

"Let your character be free from
the love of money, being content
with what you have." Heb. 13:5

*Be happy and make the most
 of what you have.*

Take time out to sit
 with your wife and
  count your blessings.

"Say to God, 'How awesome are
Thy works!'" Ps. 66:3

Tell him you appreciate all of his hard work.

Pull your wife close and
tell her she is precious.

"Rejoice in the wife of your youth." Prov. 5:18

For Him

45

Look for the rainbows;
don't always
point out the clouds.

Cherish each new day together.
Treat it as special
as the first day you met.

*Hold each other close
at least once a day.*

Place your wife at the top
of your priorities, and let
her know she's at the top.

For Him

Say "I love you" at least
once a day —
even when you are upset.

Tell your wife often that you are
thankful for her.

Live today, but dream of the future together.

Hold your wife close as you plan for the days ahead.

"When you see this, your heart will rejoice and you will flourish like grass." Isa. 66:14

For Him

49

"But let it be the hidden person of the heart, with the imperishable quality of a gentle and quiet spirit, which is precious in the sight of God." 1 Pet. 3:4

Let your husband know that his gentleness is your strength.

Just as a rose is tender and beautiful, so is your wife. Treat her as such.

"The Lord's bond-servant must . . . be kind to all." 2 Tim. 2:24

"For this cause a man shall leave his father
and his mother, and shall cleave to his wife;
and they shall become one flesh." Gen. 2:24

Marriage is a unique union of
two becoming one, his becoming
mine, me becoming we.

Do not think in terms of "mine;"
rather think in terms of "ours."

"When you do things, do not let
selfishness or pride be your
guide." Phil. 2:3; NCV

For Him

51

"Let marriage be held in
honor among all." Heb. 13:4

Your husband is yours and
yours alone. Treat him as
though he is the only one.

Your wife's wishes should
take priority over all others.

"It is good and pleasant when God's
people live in peace." Ps. 133:1; NCV

Always be giving and kind. Your husband will respond to your love with generosity.

Do not be jealous.

"Wrath is fierce and anger is a flood, but who can stand before jealousy?" Prov. 27:4

For Him

53

"Love each other . . . and take delight in honoring each other." Rom. 12:10; NIV

Never let one day go by without telling him "I love you."

Let your wife know every day how thankful you are for her. She loves to hear compliments.

"Your love is so sweet . . . my bride. Your love is better than wine." Song of Sol. 4:10; NCV

Allow your husband to show you he is a gentleman. He likes doing that.

Open the car door for your wife.

For Him

For *Her*

"Love . . . does not seek its own." 1 Cor. 13:5

Don't keep score with your husband. Be willing to give far more than you receive. The rewards will be great.

Expect to give more than you get.

"It is more blessed to give than to receive." Acts 20:35

"It is better to live in a corner of a
roof than in a house shared with a
contentious woman." Prov. 21:9

Chicken soup prepared with love means
more to your husband than a fancy
dinner prepared in anger.

Small kindnesses done
    every day mean far more to
        her than one expensive gift.

"And the seed whose fruit is
Righteousness is sown in peace by
those who make peace." James 3:18

For Him

Keep yourself looking pretty.
Use his favorite perfume.

Be neat and clean with yourself.

*Do not make plans before
checking with your husband.
Remember — you're a team.*

Do not invite dinner guests
home without first asking.

"A man who flatters his
neighbor is spreading a net
for his steps." Prov. 29:5

For Him

59

"Better is a dish of vegetables
where love is, than a fattened ox
and hatred with it." Prov. 15:17

Serve your husband's
favorite meal once a month.
Season it with love.

Help with the cleanup of
dishes without being asked.

"There is a right time and a right way
for everything." Eccles. 8:6; NCV

"I hold on to him and would not let him go." Song of Sol. 3:4

Hold hands during a movie.

Continue to treat your wife
as though you were still dating.

"Be happy with the wife you married when you were young. She gives you joy, as your fountain gives you water." Prov. 5:18; NCV

Tell your husband all the little things that are important to you. He really wants to know.

Tell your wife where you can be reached when you are away. This is important to her.

Be innovative with your finances. Learn to stretch a little to go a long way.

Never make the
financial decisions alone.

*Love your husband's family.
They will always be an
important part of his life.*

Never put down your
mother-in-law.

"Honor your father and your mother." Exod. 20:12

64

Don't compare your husband to
your father. Tell your husband
how special he alone is.

Don't compare your wife's cooking
to your mother's.

"Do not judge, lest you
be judged." Matt. 7:1

For Him

65

Learn to say "thank you" for the little things. Your husband loves to hear these words.

Help your wife with
the house cleaning.

Marriage is work, but work can bring extreme pleasure.

Be responsible.

67

"Just as the Lord forgave you, so also should you." Col. 3:13

Once something is forgiven, never mention it
to your husband again.

Hold your temper and your tongue.

"Foolish people lose their tempers, but wise people control theirs." Prov. 29:11; NCV

Treat your husband as your hero.
He likes to be your protector.

Treat your wife with respect. Remember
— she is your precious jewel.

For Him

69

Do all you can to make your home pleasing and inviting to your husband.

Do not bring your buddies home to "hang out" every night.

"Let no one seek his own good." 1 Cor. 10:24

"Wanting more is useless — like chasing after the wind." Eccles. 6:9; NCV

Comparing husbands is like comparing homes; everybody else's seems better, but very rarely is.

Never compare your wife to others. She is your special gift; love her as such.

"I am my beloved's and my beloved is mine." Song of Sol. 6:3

For Him

71

"Pleasant words are a honeycomb, sweet to the soul and healing to the bones." Prov. 16:24

Greet your husband with the positives of the day.
Save the negatives for later.

Don't bring work problems home.
Leave them at the work place.

"Don't always think about what you will eat or what you will drink, and don't keep worrying." Luke 12:29; NCV

Kiss and make up soon
after an argument.
Learn to forgive and forget.

Do not carry arguments forward
into another day.

Don't insist on always getting your own way. Learn the art of compromise.

Just as a rose is tender
and beautiful, so is your
wife. Treat her as such.

"A man's discretion makes him slow
to anger, and it is his glory to
overlook a transgression." Prov. 19:11

*A happy heart sees his good, and
overlooks the small irritations.*

A joyful heart helps your eyes
to see her beauty.

"Be happy with the wife you
married when you were young. She
gives you joy." Prov. 5:18; NCV

For Him

75

For Her

*Be flexible. Adjust to
hardships knowing that
together you'll make it.*

When plans don't work,

create new dreams together.

*Enjoy the surprises
and wonders
of each new day together.*

Put a little Christmas magic into each day. Your marriage will stay fresh as new-fallen snow.

For Him

For *Her*

"A soothing tongue is a tree of life." Prov. 15:4

When he's having
an off day, lighten the
moment with a smile.

Love your wife
through a bad mood.

"Husbands, love your wives, and do not be embittered against them." Col. 3:19

Plan a "thankful night" together and name everything you love about your husband.

Count your many blessings. You will be reminded of the happiness she brings you.

For Him

"Again I say to you that if two of you agree on earth concerning anything that they ask, it will be done for them by My Father in heaven." Matt. 18:19

Prayer is the glue that holds the two of you together.

Pray together.

"Devote yourselves to prayer, keeping alert in it with an attitude of thanksgiving." Col. 4:2

"And they who dwell . . . in earth stand in awe of Thy signs; Thou dost make the dawn and the sunset shout for joy." Ps. 65:8

Watch a sunrise together.
You will be given
fresh, new hope.

Take time away
from work to
enjoy a sunrise
with your wife.

"What the eyes see is better than what the soul desires." Eccles. 6:9

For Him

"When you talk, do not say harmful
things but say what people need —
words that will help others become
stronger." Eph. 4:29; NCV

Place an occasional love note in
your husband's lunch.

Bring home a small gift for your
wife — just because she's special.

"Do not merely look out for your own personal
interests, but also for the interests of others. Phil. 2:4

Take a break away with your husband
with absolutely nothing special on the
agenda except spending time together.

Plan a mini break away
for just the two of you. Get
to know each other again.

"Come with me . . . my bride."
Song of Sol. 4:8; NCV

For Him

83

"My husband is dazzling and ruddy, outstanding among ten thousand." *Song of Sol. 5:10*

Tell your husband he is handsome. He loves to hear those words from you.

Compliment your wife in her new outfit. She's dressing just for you!

"You are altogether beautiful, my darling, and there is no blemish in you." *Song of Sol. 4:7*

"Love . . . bears all things, believes all things, endures all things." 1 Cor. 13:4–7

Tell your husband you love him
— even on those days when he
seems to do everything wrong.

Love your wife through
a problem. She needs your
strength and support.

"Be quick to hear, slow to speak, and slow to anger." James 1:19

For Him

"Two people are better than one,
because they get more done by working
together." Eccles. 4:9; NCV

*Find one hobby that you
enjoy doing together — just
the two of you.*

Spend at least one hour a week
with your wife
working on a shared project.

"We should love not only with words and talk, but by
our actions and true caring." 1 John 3:18; NCV

"Lift up your eyes on high, and see who has created these stars. . . He calls them all by name; because of the greatness of His might and the strength of His power not one of them is missing." Isa. 40:26

Kiss your husband

under the stars.

Put a blanket on the lawn
and spend an evening
watching the stars together.

"Furthermore, if two lie down together, they keep warm, but how can one be warm alone?" Eccles. 4:11

For Him

"Your heart will be where your
treasure is." Matt. 6:21

Hearts that
share dreams together
stay together.

A single rose given
in love
holds a thousand dreams.

"Do not say, 'Why is it that the former days
were better than these?'" Eccles. 7:10

Be your husband's greatest sports fan. Many times he will stand alone, except for having you.

Love your wife
even when she
feels unlovely.

For Him

"Let's go early to the vineyards . . .
let's see if the blossoms have already
opened." Song of Sol. 7:12; NCV

*Be spontaneous.
Grab his hand and splash through
the mud puddles together.*

Take your wife on a
romantic walk in the rain.
Kiss under the raindrops.

"Your lips are like a scarlet thread, and
your mouth is lovely." Song of Sol. 4:3

Buy a small gift for him when he least expects it.

Surprise her with a bottle of her favorite perfume.

For Him

*Fall asleep holding hands.
You'll keep his heart warm.*

Rub her cold feet before bed.
She'll love you forever!

Tell him you're sorry.
His heart will melt.

Kiss and make up.
It's no fun being
angry at each other.

For *Her*

"He has made everything beautiful in its time." Eccles. 3:11; NIV

Stroll along the beach hand in hand watching the rolling waves. Your love will be renewed.

Take a quiet walk along the beach with the one you love. You will be reminded how precious she truly is.

"Come and see the works of God, who is awesome in His deed toward the sons of men." Ps. 66:5

Always keep your bedroom fresh, neat, and inviting.

Cherish

quiet

moments

together.

"Who is she who looks for as the morning, fair as the moon, clear as the sun?" Song of Sol. 6:10; NIV

For Him

95

"Those who are careful about what they say keep themselves out of trouble." Prov. 21:23; NCV

PMS week is the wrong week to exercise your vocal chords. **Practice Mostly Silence.**

Never say aloud
everything that you feel.

"Like apples of gold in settings of silver is a word spoken in right circumstances." Prov. 25:11

Never make fun of your
husband's insecurities. Instead,
compliment your husband to others.

Tell others of your wife's good points.
The rest is private and
should be kept that way.

For Him

For *Her*

"With patience you can convince
a ruler, and a gentle word can get
through to the hard-headed."
Prov. 25:15; NCV

*Learn how to
handle frustration or
frustration will handle you.*

Patience takes care of more problems in a
marriage than anger. Learn to practice
patience with your wife.

"Love is patient. . . ." 1 Cor. 13:4

Remember the peaks to help you through the valleys.

When hardships come knocking at your door, remember the beautiful moments you've shared together. Tender memories will keep your love strong.

"Whatever is lovely . . . let your mind dwell on these things." Phil. 4:8

For Him

99

For Her

"Before I realized it, my desire for you made me feel like a prince in a chariot." Song of Sol. 6:12; NCV

Men think differently than women. Accept this as a gift, rather than a problem.

You will never completely understand her. That's part of God's wonderful design.

"She shall be called woman because she was taken out of man." Gen. 2:23

100

*Give more than fifty percent.
Marriage takes your "all."*

There are no dividing lines in a marriage. Remember — you are partners with the same goal in mind.

"For I have learned to be
content in whatever
circumstances I am." Phil. 4:11

When the sun isn't shining, learn to sing together in the rain.

Sometimes you have to live with the clouds
and learn to be thankful for them.

"Consider it all joy . . . when you encounter
various trials, knowing that the testing of your
faith produces endurance." James 1:2–3

"And he will be like a tree firmly planted by streams of water, which yield fruit in due season." Ps. 1:3

Your life together is an adventure for every season. Spend time with your husband enjoying the stops along the way.

Marriage is an exciting journey.
Take time with your wife to
smell the roses along the way.

"I will praise the Lord while I live; I will sing praises to my God while I have my being." Ps. 146:2

"Bright eyes gladden the heart." Prov. 15:30

Look deep into his eyes, for it is there you will see his heart.

Tell her she has beautiful eyes.
Her heart will fill with joy.

"How beautiful you are! Your eyes are like doves." Song of Sol. 4:1

You can work through any
problem together when
love is your guide.

Allow love for your wife
    to be the determining factor
        in solving any problem.

"For not one of us lives for himself, and not one dies for himself." Rom. 14:7

Time spent together is never time wasted. It helps keep your love strong.

Make time to spend alone with your wife. The closer you are, the closer you will become.

"A man who has just married . . . should be free to stay home for a year to make his new wife happy." Deut. 24:5; NCV

*Work can wait;
your husband's heart needs you now.*

Hold your wife close today. She needs to know you consider her more important than your work.

For Him

"Many are the afflictions of the righteous; but the Lord delivers him out of them all." Ps. 34:19

Remind yourself often that tough times in marriage never last forever.

Your love for her will grow
even in the midst of
difficulties and pain.

"Hope deferred makes the heart sick, but a longing fulfilled is a tree of life." Prov. 13:12; NIV

Be creative.
Plan a romantic
indoor picnic by candlelight.

Camp out in front of the
    fireplace together. You'll capture
        the joy of being kids again.

When you speak gently,
he will never tune you out.

Kind words will
always keep
her attention.

Nagging will never draw you close together. Tell him how you feel using positive words, instead.

Say what's on your mind gently.
If that doesn't work,
then begin changing yourself.

"When there are many words, transgression is unavoidable, but he who restrains his lips is wise." Prov. 10:19

For Him

111

"Your neck is like the tower of David, built with rows of stones, on which are hung a thousand shields . . . of the mighty men." Song of Sol. 4:4

Think of him as
your tower of strength
anchored to God,
motivated by love.

Picture your wife as a lily —
gracefully adorned by God himself.

"Like a lily among the thorns, so is my darling among the maidens." Song of Sol. 2:2

Stretch out in the
soft meadow grass
together.

Take time to relax, let all cares drift
away, and simply enjoy being in the
presence of your wife.

"Look at the birds of the air. . . .
Are you not worth much more
than they?" Matt. 6:26

For Him

113

For *Her*

"I am my beloved's, and his desire is
toward me." Song of Sol. 7:10; KJV

His presence fills the rooms of your
heart with love. Tell him how very
much you love it when he is near.

Your wife is like the fragrance of a
wonderfully scented potpourri that fills
your home. Take time to enjoy the aroma.

"How beautiful is your love, my sister, my bride! How
much better is your love than wine, and the fragrance of
your oils than all kinds of spices." Song of Sol. 4:10

Always pull
together on
major issues.

Learn to compromise.
Many problems take
some giving on both sides.

"He who guards his mouth and his tongue, guards his soul from troubles." Prov. 21:23

For Him

115

"Spoken words can be like deep water . . . wisdom is like a flowing stream." Prov. 18:4; NCV

Save your most cherished thoughts for your husband. He loves when you whisper secrets in his ear.

Be your
wife's best friend.

"It is better to eat a dry crust of bread in peace than to have a feast where there is quarreling." Prov. 17:1; NCV

A little lace, perfume, and soft music will bring romance back into your marriage.

Sometimes it takes your imagination
to live romantically.
Buy some flowers and scented candles.

For Her

*"Love patiently accepts all things.
It always trusts, always hopes,
and always remains strong."
1 Cor. 13:7; NCV*

*The man you married is
completely unique.
Cherish his differences.*

Treat your wife as an endangered
species. Remember — she's special,
one of a kind, and irreplaceable!

*"Her husband praises her, saying, 'There are
many fine women, but you are better than all
of them.'" Prov. 31:28; NCV*

Crying doesn't mean you're not in love.
It simply means you are going through
some major adjustments.

Most wives cry a lot the first year.
Tenderly dry her tears.

"But encourage one another
day after day." Heb. 3:13

For Him

119

"I love the Lord because He listens to my prayers." Ps. 116:1; NCV

Whisper a prayer together every morning.

Hold her hand
and close the
day in prayer.

"Pray without ceasing." 1 Thess. 5:17

Create traditions early in your
marriage. You will have a treasure
of precious memories to
share in the years to come.

Holiday traditions are fun. Help your
wife decide on traditions that will make
fond remembrances for the two of you.

"And He came to Nazareth, where
He had been brought up; and as
was His custom." Luke 4:16

For Him

"A cheerful look brings joy to the heart, and good news gives health to the bones." Prov. 15:30; NIV

Make laughter part of your everyday living. When you're happy, your husband will be, too.

Laugh with your
wife at least
once every day.

"A joyful heart makes a cheerful face, but when the heart is sad, the spirit is broken." Prov. 15:13

"I am the Rose of Sharon, the lily of the valleys." Song of Sol. 2:1

Surprise your
husband with
a new hairstyle.

Notice your wife's new make-up,
hairstyle, and outfit.
She's doing it for you!

"You have thrilled my heart with a glance of your eyes, with one sparkle from your necklace." Song of Sol. 4:9; NCV

For Him

"A gift in secret subdues anger." Prov. 22:14

Surprise him with
    a gift from his
        personal wish list.

When buying her a gift, use
    your heart and not your head.

"The generous man will be prosperous, and he who waters will himself be watered." Prov. 11:25

The better you feel about
yourself, the easier it is to love
him. Replenish yourself often.

Loving yourself is loving her.

"Pleasant words are a honeycomb, sweet to the soul and healing to the bones." Prov. 17:7

Warm words take the chill
out of a cold evening.

Giving her
an unexpected hug
will break the ice.

"Go then, eat your bread of happiness, and drink your wine with a cheerful heart." Eccles. 9:7

Snuggle under a blanket together.

Hot chocolate and a warm muffin served in bed will warm her heart.

The Fragrance of Love

Dan and Dave Davidson

This delightful book is packed with quips, quotations and quiet moments all centered around the theme of love. Packaged with fragrant potpourri, it becomes the perfect gift of love for anyone, anytime.

ISBN: 0-89221- 513-5 • $8.99
(includes 3.5 oz. box of potpourri)

Book only: **ISBN:** 0-89221-509-7 • $5.99

Available at Christian bookstores nationwide